Math Splash

Help the frog get to the pond by solving the problem on each rock.

Don't forget to regroup when you need to.

$$\begin{array}{r} 38 \\ +15 \\ \hline 53 \end{array}$$

$$\begin{array}{r} 47 \\ -18 \\ \hline \end{array}$$

$$\begin{array}{r} 19 \\ +34 \\ \hline \end{array}$$

$$\begin{array}{r} 90 \\ -51 \\ \hline \end{array}$$

$$\begin{array}{r} 58 \\ -42 \\ \hline \end{array}$$

$$\begin{array}{r} 44 \\ +26 \\ \hline \end{array}$$

$$\begin{array}{r} 24 \\ +55 \\ \hline \end{array}$$

$$\begin{array}{r} 23 \\ -17 \\ \hline \end{array}$$

$$\begin{array}{r} 41 \\ -21 \\ \hline \end{array}$$

$$\begin{array}{r} 63 \\ +37 \\ \hline \end{array}$$

Four at a Time

Add.

When adding more than two numbers, look for easy combinations first.

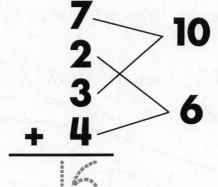 

$$
\begin{array}{r} 6 \\ 8 \\ 2 \\ + 4 \\ \hline \end{array}
\qquad
\begin{array}{r} 3 \\ 3 \\ 3 \\ + 7 \\ \hline \end{array}
\qquad
\begin{array}{r} 5 \\ 5 \\ 2 \\ + 3 \\ \hline \end{array}
\qquad
\begin{array}{r} 1 \\ 6 \\ 9 \\ + 5 \\ \hline \end{array}
\qquad
\begin{array}{r} 2 \\ 9 \\ 4 \\ + 8 \\ \hline \end{array}
$$

$$
\begin{array}{r} 4 \\ 6 \\ 8 \\ + 0 \\ \hline \end{array}
\qquad
\begin{array}{r} 7 \\ 7 \\ 5 \\ + 3 \\ \hline \end{array}
\qquad
\begin{array}{r} 3 \\ 9 \\ 1 \\ + 1 \\ \hline \end{array}
\qquad
\begin{array}{r} 4 \\ 3 \\ 6 \\ + 4 \\ \hline \end{array}
\qquad
\begin{array}{r} 9 \\ 8 \\ 7 \\ + 2 \\ \hline \end{array}
$$

$$
\begin{array}{r} 5 \\ 5 \\ 5 \\ + 5 \\ \hline \end{array}
\qquad
\begin{array}{r} 6 \\ 6 \\ 4 \\ + 3 \\ \hline \end{array}
\qquad
\begin{array}{r} 3 \\ 7 \\ 8 \\ + 5 \\ \hline \end{array}
\qquad
\begin{array}{r} 7 \\ 7 \\ 7 \\ + 7 \\ \hline \end{array}
\qquad
\begin{array}{r} 4 \\ 8 \\ 8 \\ + 4 \\ \hline \end{array}
$$

Adding four 1-digit numbers

Number Sleuth

Solve the riddles.

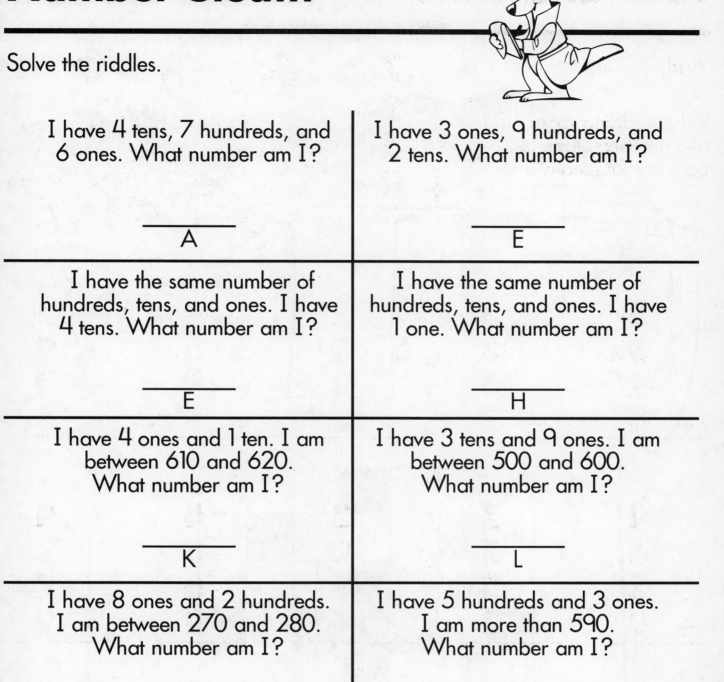

I have 4 tens, 7 hundreds, and 6 ones. What number am I?

_____
A

I have 3 ones, 9 hundreds, and 2 tens. What number am I?

_____
E

I have the same number of hundreds, tens, and ones. I have 4 tens. What number am I?

_____
E

I have the same number of hundreds, tens, and ones. I have 1 one. What number am I?

_____
H

I have 4 ones and 1 ten. I am between 610 and 620. What number am I?

_____
K

I have 3 tens and 9 ones. I am between 500 and 600. What number am I?

_____
L

I have 8 ones and 2 hundreds. I am between 270 and 280. What number am I?

_____
O

I have 5 hundreds and 3 ones. I am more than 590. What number am I?

_____
Y

Match the numbers with letters above to answer the riddle.

What goes through a door, but never goes in or out?

_____ 746   _____ 614   _____ 923   _____ 593   _____ 111   _____ 278   _____ 539   _____ 444

Sum Castle

Write the sum for each clue.

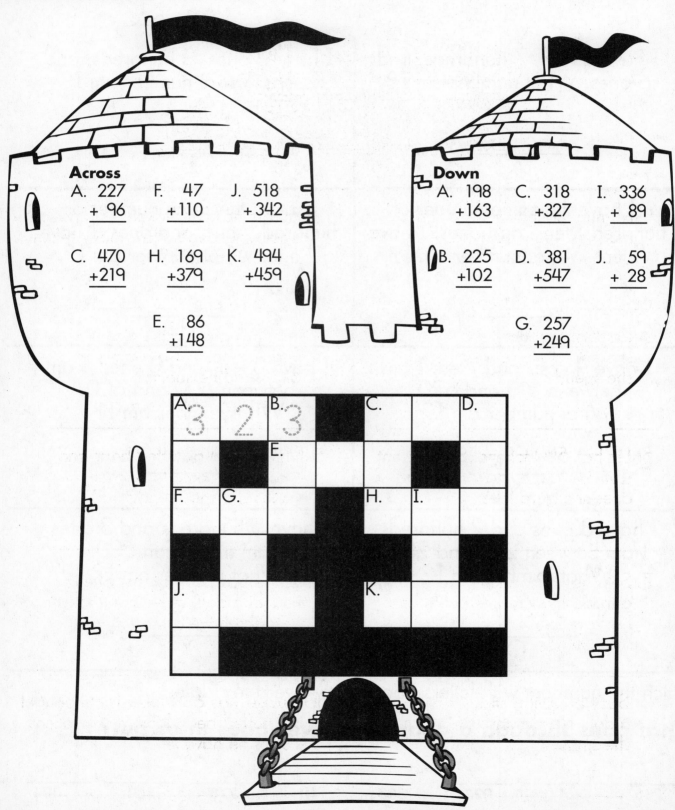

Across

A. 227
   + 96

C. 470
   +219

E.   86
   +148

F.   47
   +110

H. 169
   +379

J. 518
   +342

K. 494
   +459

Down

A. 198
   +163

B. 225
   +102

C. 318
   +327

D. 381
   +547

G. 257
   +249

I. 336
   + 89

J.   59
   + 28

Adding 3-digit numbers

Token Trade In

Read each problem. Write a number sentence and solve.

1. Manuel bought a truck and markers. How many tokens did he spend?

_____

2. Hunter has 390 tokens. He bought a coloring book. How many tokens does he have left?

_____

3. Kameisha bought a doll and stickers. How many tokens did she spend?

_____

4. Nick bought stickers and a sticker book. How many tokens did he spend?

_____

5. Liz has 540 tokens. She bought a sticker book. How many tokens does she have left?

_____

6. Mai bought a stuffed bear and a coloring book. How many tokens did she spend?

_____

7. Seth has 425 tokens. He bought a truck. How many tokens does he have left?

_____

8. Jenna has 350 tokens. She bought a doll. How many tokens does she have left?

_____

9. Suzy bought a sticker book and a doll. How many tokens did she spend?

_____

10. Tucker has 639 tokens. He bought a stuffed bear. How many tokens does he have left?

_____

Dive Into Numbers

Write the number.

5000 + 200 + 10 + 7 = _____

7000 + 100 + 70 + 4 = _____

8000 + 700 + 20 + 6 = _____

4000 + 400 + 60 + 2 = _____

9000 + 900 + 40 + 8 = _____

Write an addition sentence.

2342 = _____ + _____ + _____ + _____

6815 = _____ + _____ + _____ + _____

1789 = _____ + _____ + _____ + _____

3603 = _____ + _____ + _____ + _____

7496 = _____ + _____ + _____ + _____

Writing 4-digit numbers

Name Game

Write the number.

One thousand, two hundred eleven = _____

Eight thousand, thirty-five = _____

Seven thousand, one hundred = _____

Five thousand, four hundred twenty-three = _____

Nine thousand, five hundred seventeen = _____

Two thousand, seven hundred thirty-four = _____

Two thousand, eight hundred nine = _____

Five thousand, three hundred forty-two = _____

Six thousand, nine hundred sixty-one = _____

Four thousand, two hundred ninety = _____

Three thousand, one hundred seventy-five = _____

Four thousand, six hundred fifty-seven = _____

Nine thousand = _____

Three thousand, four hundred thirty-two = _____

Four thousand, two hundred nine = _____

Adding Thousands

Add. Circle the sums that are greater than 6000. What pattern do you see?

```
  2346        2935        3024        4147
+ 3754      + 1263      + 3126      + 2053
──────
  6100
```

```
  3152        3125        1246        1168
+ 1756      + 3125      + 1725      + 5132
```

```
  2132        3049        5143        2914
+ 4218      + 2743      + 1257      + 2279
```

```
  4373        1221        2936        4680
+ 1612      + 5229      + 3564      + 1299
```

```
  3035        1794        2605        4237
+ 3515      + 1179      + 2236      + 2363
```

Adding 4-digit numbers

Subtracting Thousands

Find the difference.

4321 − 1218	5619 − 2804	9846 − 4373	6527 − 2213
3103			

7049 − 3528	3267 − 1742	8473 − 2439	5742 − 1812

6836 − 2724	2799 − 1982	4954 − 1426	7821 − 2816

5431 − 2161	8862 − 1215	3961 − 2820	9789 − 3299

3776 − 1349	7449 − 2623	6675 − 2231	5859 − 4182

Odds and Evens

Color the **odd** numbered balls blue.
Color the **even** numbered balls yellow.

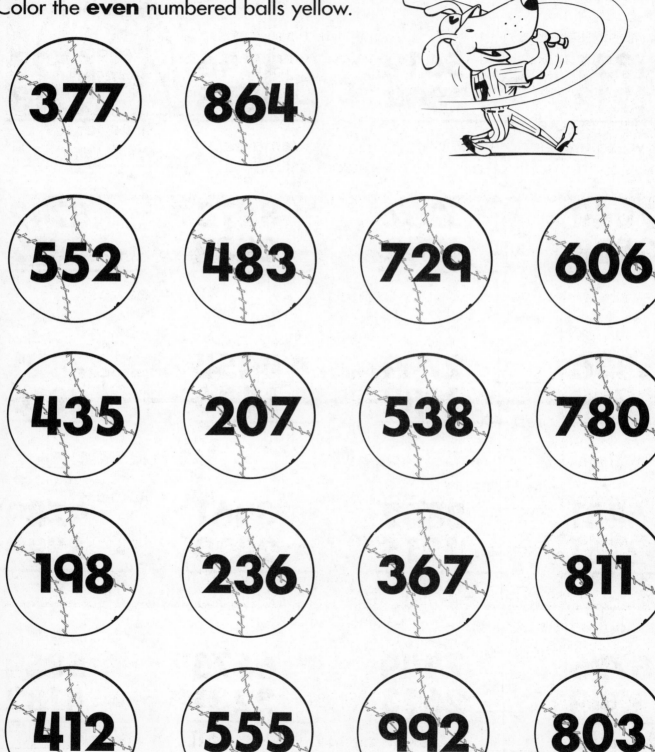

377   864

552   483   729   606

435   207   538   780

198   236   367   811

412   555   992   803

Identifying odd and even numbers

Rounding Numbers

First, find the place value that you are rounding to. Then, look at the number immediately to the right.

If the number to the right is 5 or more, increase the place value number by one and make the remaining numbers to the right zeros.   **16 becomes 20**

If the number to the right is 4 or less, keep the place value number the same and make the remaining numbers to the right zeros.   **14 becomes 10**

5 or more, let it soar!

4 or less, let it rest!

Round to the nearest 10.

54 = almost _50_   **91** = almost _____   **64** = almost _____

69 = almost _____   **82** = almost _____   **88** = almost _____

33 = almost _____   **28** = almost _____   **37** = almost _____

76 = almost _____   **45** = almost _____   **99** = almost _____

Round to the nearest 100.

652 = almost _700_   **481** = almost _____   **522** = almost _____

320 = almost _____   **768** = almost _____   **149** = almost _____

805 = almost _____   **916** = almost _____   **674** = almost _____

163 = almost _____   **290** = almost _____   **358** = almost _____

Round to the nearest 1000.

5263 = almost _5000_   **2981** = almost_____   **9237** = almost_____

7891 = almost_____   **3496** = almost_____   **5509** = almost_____

1026 = almost_____   **8804** = almost_____   **6112** = almost_____

6549 = almost_____   **4175** = almost_____   **2466** = almost_____

Measuring Cups and Spoons

1 cup = 2 half cups 1 tablespoon (tbsp.) = 3 teaspoons (tsp.)

Color the cups to show the same amount.

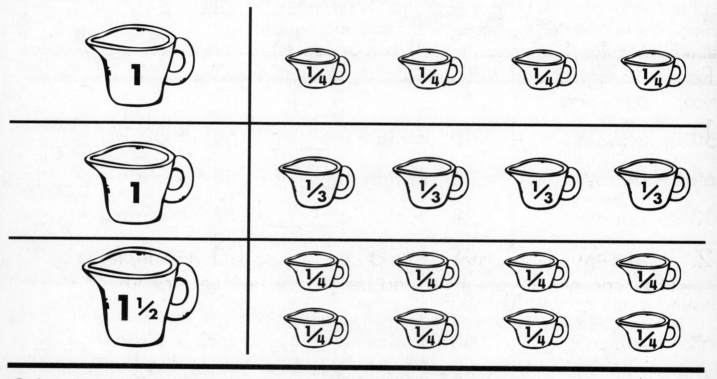

Color the spoons to show the same amount.

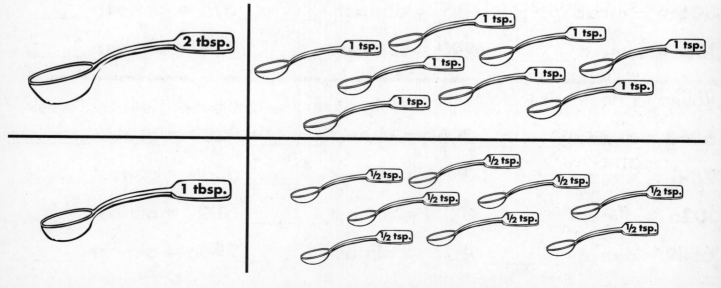

Understanding liquid measurement

Pounds and Ounces

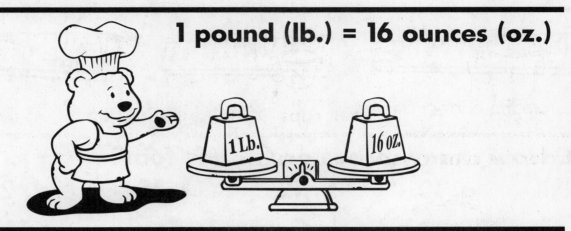

1 pound (lb.) = 16 ounces (oz.)

Read each problem. Then use addition or subtraction to solve it.

1. Mary made four 16-ounce cakes. How many pounds of cake did she make?

2. It takes two pounds of ground beef to make Jeff's meatloaf. How many ounces of ground beef does he need to buy?

3. Julie's guinea pig weighs 56 ounces. How many pounds does the guinea pig weigh?

4. Zack's backpack weighs 48 ounces. He removed his math book, which weighs one pound. How much does his backpack weigh now?

Feet, Yards, and Meters

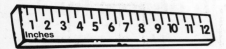  

Circle the correct answer.

1. How many inches are in one foot?

     a. 10   b. 12   c. 15   d. 24

2. How many feet are in one yard?

     a. 4   b. 2   c. 3   d. 5

3. How many centimeters are in one meter?

     a. 100   b. 50   c. 10   d. 200

4. How many inches are in one yard?

     a. 34   b. 24   c. 12   d. 36

Write the answers.

1. How many feet are in 3 yards? _____

2. How many inches are in 3 feet? _____

3. How many inches are in 2 yards? _____

4. How many centimeters are in 5 meters? _____

5. How many feet are in 4 yards? _____

     Understanding linear measurements

Same Size

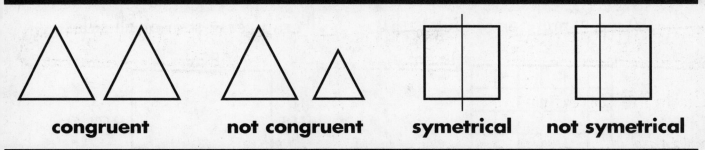

congruent   not congruent   symetrical   not symetrical

Circle the correct answer.

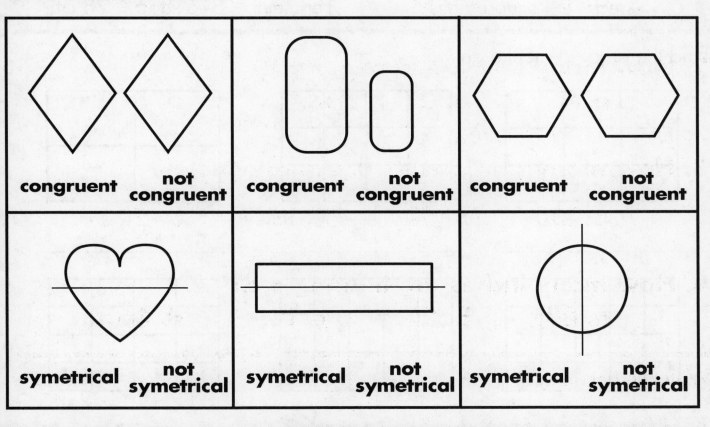

congruent   not congruent   congruent   not congruent   congruent   not congruent

symetrical   not symetrical   symetrical   not symetrical   symetrical   not symetrical

Draw two congruent shapes.

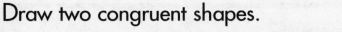

Divide the shape symmetrically.

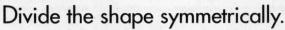

Area and Perimeter

Area = number of units

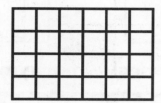

Area = 24 square units

Perimeter = sum of all sides

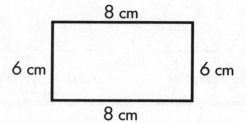

Perimeter = 8+6+8+6 = 28 cm.

Find the area. Write the answer.

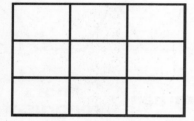

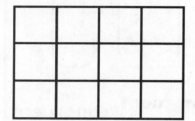

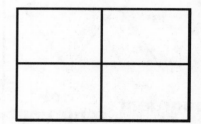

_____

_____

_____

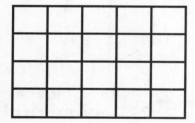

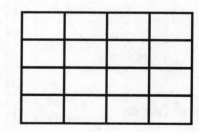

_____

_____

_____

Find the perimeter. Write the answer.

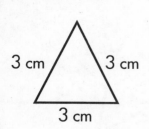

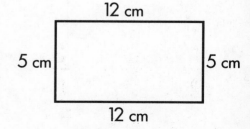

_____

_____

_____

Determining area and perimeter

Comparing Fractions

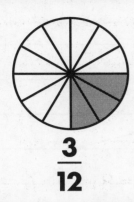

$\dfrac{3}{12}$

=

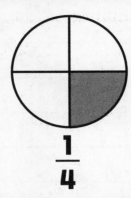

$\dfrac{1}{4}$

Write the fraction to show what part is shaded.

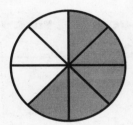

_____

_____

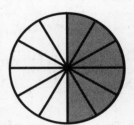

_____

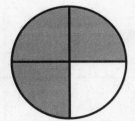

_____

_____

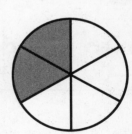

_____

Rewrite the fractions in order from smallest to largest.

$\dfrac{1}{4}$ $\dfrac{2}{12}$ $\dfrac{1}{2}$ $\dfrac{3}{8}$ $\dfrac{2}{3}$ ____ ____ ____ ____ ____

How's the Weather?

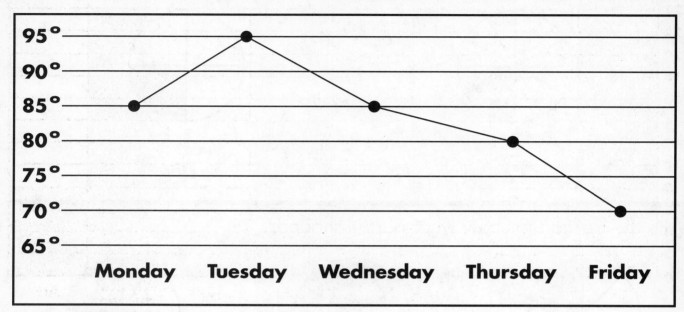

Use the graph to answer the questions.

1. What was the temperature on Wednesday?

_____

2. Which two days had the same temperature?

_____

3. Which day had the highest temperature?

_____

4. Which day had the lowest temperature?

_____

5. How many days was the temperature recorded?

_____

Favorite Subject

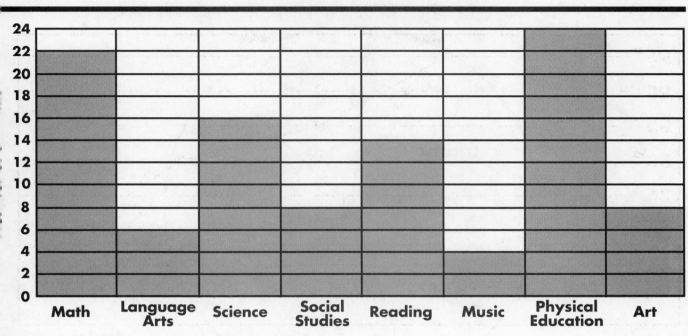

Use the graph to answer the questions.

. How many students said science was their favorite subject? _____

2. Which was the most favorite subject?

_____

3. Which was the least favorite subject?

_____

4. Which two subjects tied?

_____

5. How many more students said math than reading?

_____

Favorite Sport

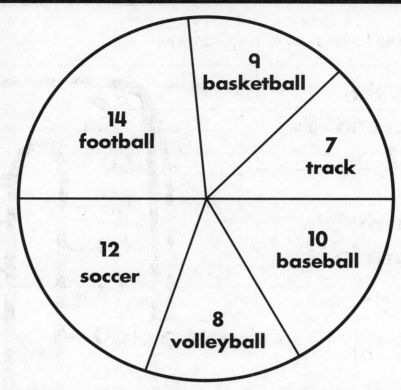

Each student named one sport. Use the graph to answer the questions.

1. Which was the most favorite sport? _____

2. Which was the least favorite sport? _____

3. How many students named a favorite sport? _____

4. How many students said volleyball? _____

5. How many more students said soccer than basketball? _____

6. What fraction of students said football? _____

Temperature

Use the thermometer to answer the questions.

1. **What was the temperature in °F at sunrise?** _____

2. **What was the temperature in °C at noon?** _____

3. **What was the temperature in °F at sunset?** _____

4. **How much warmer (°F) was it at sunset than it was at sunrise?** _____

5. **Is 0°C warmer than 20°F?** _____

6. **Is 20°C colder than 50°F?** _____

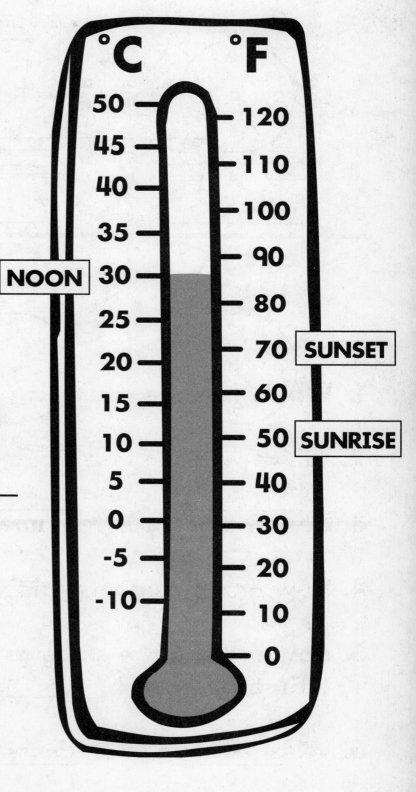

Robot Time

Write the time.

7:32

__:__   __:__   __:__

__:__   __:__   __:__

   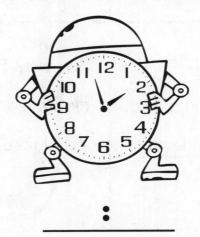   

__:__   __:__   __:__

Summer Time Fun

Read each problem. Write the answer.

Eric left home at 11 o'clock.

It took 1½ hours to get to the beach.

What time did Eric get to the beach?

_____

Kate goes to camp at 11 a.m.

Pat goes to camp at 1 p.m.

Who goes to camp first?

_____

Samir got to the park at 2:45 p.m.

He went home at 5 p.m.

How long was Samir at the park?

_____

The soccer game starts at 6 o'clock.

It ends one and a quarter hours later.

What time does the soccer game end?

_____

Meg left home at 9 o'clock.

It took her 2½ hours to get to Aunt Lynn's.

What time did Meg get to Aunt Lynn's?

Ben went to the pool at 2:00.

He stayed for 3 hours and 35 minutes.

What time did Ben go home?

In the Bank

Count the money. Write the amount.

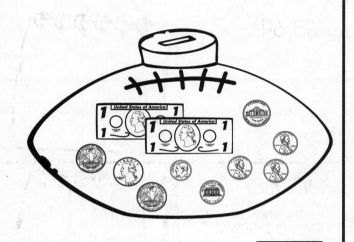

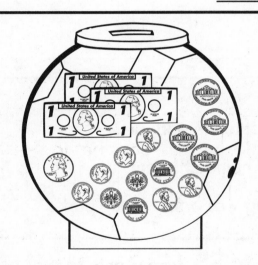

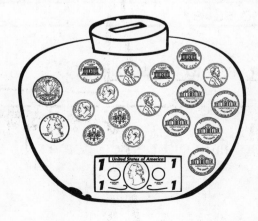

Counting money

How Much Money?

Solve the problems.

Rosa has $10.00. She bought a dress for $8.64. How much money does she have left?

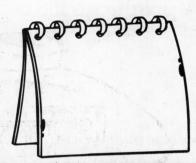

_____

Howard has $7.50. He wants to buy a video that costs $9.00. How much money does he need to save?

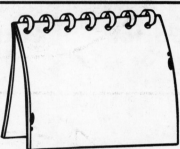

_____

Todd has $8.78. He bought a football for $7.97. How much money does he have left?

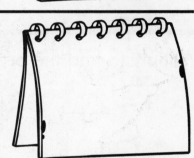

_____

Jill has $6.85. She wants to buy a purse that costs $10.00. How much money does she need to save?

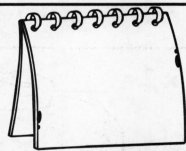

_____

Paul has $9.20. He bought a hat for $5.91. How much money does he have left?

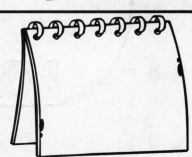

_____

Put a Name to the Number

Factors are the numbers you use to multiply.
A **product** is the answer you get when you multiply factors together.

Factor	Factor	Product
2	x 3	= 6

Whenever you multiply a factor by the number 1,
the product is equal to that factor.

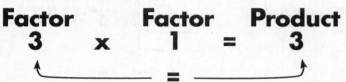

"Perfect! I won't change a single thing about it."

Multiply to find the product.

1 x 9 = ___   2 x 1 = ___   1 x 5 = ___   7 x 1 = ___

3 x 1 = ___   1 x 1 = ___   4 x 2 = ___   9 x 1 = ___

8 x 1 = ___   2 x 2 = ___   1 x 4 = ___   2 x 6 = ___

1 x 2 = ___   5 x 2 = ___   6 x 1 = ___   7 x 2 = ___

2 x 8 = ___   1 x 8 = ___   1 x 3 = ___   1 x 6 = ___

3 x 2 = ___   9 x 2 = ___   5 x 1 = ___   2 x 7 = ___

Understanding multiplication; practicing multiplication facts

Find the Perfect Fit

Write the missing factors.

$\underline{}$ x 3 = 12   6 x $\underline{}$ = 18   4 x $\underline{}$ = 16

$\underline{}$ x 9 = 27 $\underline{}$ x 5 = 20   3 x $\underline{}$ = 9

6 x $\underline{}$ = 24 $\underline{}$ x 3 = 15 $\underline{}$ x 3 = 24

$\underline{}$ x 4 = 36   3 x $\underline{}$ = 21   3 x $\underline{}$ = 6

"I did all that multiplying for nothing, nada, zip, ZERO!"

In multiplication, any number multiplied by zero equals zero and zero multiplied by any number equals zero.

$$A \times 0 = 0 \text{ and } 0 \times A = 0$$
$$3 \times 0 = \text{no 3s} = 0$$
$$0 \times 3 = 0 + 0 + 0 = 0$$

Multiply.

7 x 0 = ___   2 x 0 = ___   0 x 5 = ___   0 x 1 = ___

0 x 6 = ___   0 x 4 = ___   3 x 0 = ___   9 x 0 = ___

8 x 0 = ___   0 x 7 = ___   6 x 0 = ___   1 x 0 = ___

Two of a Kind

In multiplication, A x B is equal to B x A.

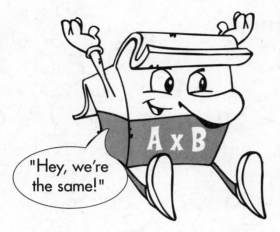

A x B = B x A   3 x 5 = 15

3 x 5 = 5 x 3   5 x 3 = 15

Rewrite the factors to show that A x B equals B x A.
Then solve the problems.

5 x 6 = ___ x ___ = ___   6 x 3 = ___ x ___ = ___

4 x 5 = ___ x ___ = ___   2 x 6 = ___ x ___ = ___

6 x 4 = ___ x ___ = ___   6 x 7 = ___ x ___ = ___

5 x 2 = ___ x ___ = ___   7 x 5 = ___ x ___ = ___

8 x 6 = ___ x ___ = ___   9 x 5 = ___ x ___ = ___

5 x 8 = ___ x ___ = ___   6 x 9 = ___ x ___ = ___

Monster Munch

Multiply. Then use the code to answer the riddle.

Why did the monster eat the lamp?

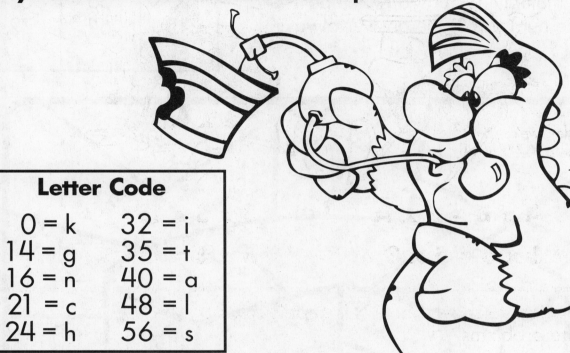

"Yum."

Letter Code	
0 = k	32 = i
14 = g	35 = t
16 = n	40 = a
21 = c	48 = l
24 = h	56 = s

He wanted a _____ .

8 x 6	4 x 8	7 x 2	8 x 3	5 x 7
48				
l				
7 x 8	2 x 8	8 x 5	3 x 7	7 x 0
				.

Tasty Times

Multiply. Then use the code to color the picture.

Tip: When multiplying 9 by any number except 0, the numbers in the answer always add up to 9.

Yellow	Pink	Green
0	9	18
27	36	63
45	54	72
81		

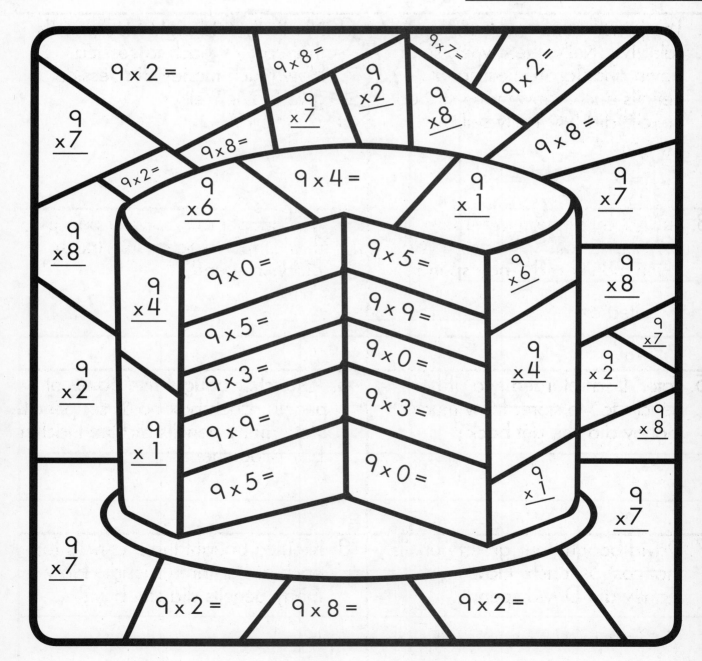

30

Practicing multiplication facts

Pencils for Sale

Read each problem then solve it using multiplication. Show your work.

1. The pencil store was having a sale. Mr. Kelly, the owner, sold Kevin and Jason six striped pencils each. How many striped pencils did Mr. Kelly sell to the boys?

2. Mr. Kelly sold eight blue pencils that cost 7¢ each to Jessica. How much money did Jessica give to Mr. Kelly?

3. Andy bought nine superhero pencils that cost 8¢ each. How much money did Andy spend?

4. Lisa bought four sparkly pencils that cost 9¢ each. How much did Lisa spend?

5. Later, Lisa returned two of her pencils to the store. How much money did she get back?

6. A teacher bought five boxes of pencils. Each box holds six pencils. How many pencils did the teacher buy altogether?

7. David bought four green pencils that cost 5¢ each. How much money did David spend?

8. Monica bought three pencils for each of her three friends. How many pencils did she buy?

All About Division

A division problem is often written one of two ways.

$$8 \div 4 = 2 \qquad 4\overline{)8}\,^{2}$$

"Name, please?"

"Well, in multiplication my name is factor...or product. 'Course, if you're talking division, it could also be quotient, or dividend or..."

The numbers used in division have special names:

divisor → (the number used to divide) $4\overline{)8}\,^{2}$ ← **quotient** (the answer)

← **dividend** (the number being divided)

dividend	divisor	quotient
8 ÷	**4** =	**2**

Write the numbers used for each division problem.

$2\overline{)6}\,^{3}$ _____ dividend   _____ divisor   _____ quotient

14 ÷ 7 = 2   _____ dividend   _____ divisor   _____ quotient

Divide.

$6\overline{)12}$ $2\overline{)2}$ $2\overline{)8}$ 6 ÷ 6 = _____

$9\overline{)18}$ $2\overline{)10}$ $1\overline{)9}$ 14 ÷ 2 = _____

$2\overline{)6}$ $5\overline{)5}$ $2\overline{)4}$ 8 ÷ 1 = _____

Quotient Match

Match each problem with its quotient.

3⟌15	5	4⟌24
4⟌20	2	3⟌21
4⟌8	6	3⟌9
3⟌18	7	4⟌16
4⟌32	3	3⟌6
4⟌28	4	4⟌12
3⟌27	8	3⟌24
	9	

Division is Tee-rrific!

Divide. Then use the code to answer the riddle.

Letter Code:

1 = i	4 = h	7 = e
2 = d	5 = l	8 = S
3 = o	6 = n	9 = a

Why did the golfer change her socks?

S		
8		
6⟌48	5⟌20	5⟌35

6⟌24	5⟌45	6⟌12

3⟌27

4⟌16	6⟌18	5⟌25	2⟌14

3⟌3	6⟌36

5⟌15	4⟌24	4⟌28

Understanding division; practicing division facts

Divissssssion!

Divide.

7⟌56   8⟌8   8⟌16

7⟌21   8⟌32   7⟌14   8⟌64   7⟌7

8⟌24   7⟌49   8⟌40   7⟌63   8⟌48

7⟌35   8⟌72   7⟌28   8⟌56   7⟌42

Match each multiplication fact with the correct division fact.

8 x 4	7⟌49
7 x 7	8⟌32
7 x 9	8⟌48
8 x 6	7⟌63
7 x 5	5⟌35

Math Mysteries

Find the quotient.

$6\overline{)54}$ $7\overline{)63}$ $9\overline{)45}$

$9\overline{)81}$ $3\overline{)27}$ $9\overline{)9}$ $2\overline{)18}$ $9\overline{)72}$

$5\overline{)45}$ $9\overline{)54}$ $4\overline{)36}$ $9\overline{)63}$ $9\overline{)27}$

Find the dividend.

$9\overline{)}^{3}$ $9\overline{)}^{6}$ $2\overline{)}^{9}$ $9\overline{)}^{8}$ $4\overline{)}^{9}$

$9\overline{)}^{9}$ $9\overline{)}^{5}$ $7\overline{)}^{9}$ $6\overline{)}^{9}$ $9\overline{)}^{1}$

Find the divisor.

$\underline{}\overline{)81}^{9}$ $\underline{}\overline{)54}^{6}$ $\underline{}\overline{)27}^{9}$ $\underline{}\overline{)72}^{8}$ $\underline{}\overline{)45}^{9}$

$\underline{}\overline{)36}^{9}$ $\underline{}\overline{)18}^{2}$ $\underline{}\overline{)9}^{9}$ $\underline{}\overline{)63}^{7}$ $\underline{}\overline{)54}^{9}$

Practicing division facts

Fun at School

Read each problem then solve it using division. Show your work.

---

1. Sarah jump roped for 21 hours in seven days. If she jumped the same amount of time every day, how many hours of jump roping did she do each day?

2. At the school fair, 42 children want to run in the egg and spoon race. Only six children can race at a time. How many races will it take for everyone to have a turn?

---

3. The school has 54 children who want to play stickball. If there can only be nine players on each team, how many teams must be formed?

4. Mrs. Williams has made 40 candy apples to sell. If she sells eight every hour, how many hours will it take for her to sell them all?

---

5. There are 36 children who want their faces painted at the fair. Mrs. Adams, the face painter, can paint nine faces in one hour. How many hours will it take for her to paint all 36 children?

6. The children in Mr. Grandy's class love sweets. The class ate 24 sticks of cotton candy! Since they ate four sticks every hour, how many hours did it take them to eat all 24?

---

7. Mrs. Winkle gave out 49 stickers to seven students. If every student was given the same number of stickers, how many did each student receive?

8. There are 18 students in the school orchestra. If every two students share one music stand, how many music stands are there altogether?

Everything in Its Place

To multiply a two-digit number by a one-digit number, arrange the numbers in columns of 100s, 10s, and 1s. You won't always need to use the 100s and 10s columns.

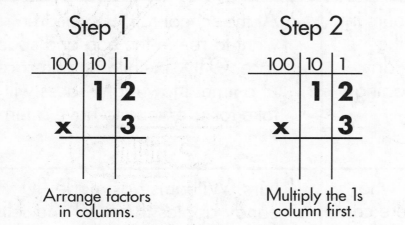

Step 1	Step 2	Step 3
Arrange factors in columns.	Multiply the 1s column first.	Then multiply the 10s column.

Rewrite the problem in columns then multiply.
Remember, multiply the 1s column then the 10s column.

11 x 5

13 x 2

12 x 3

10 x 4

12 x 4

14 x 2

One Column at a Time

Multiply.

14 x 2	31 x 3	44 x 2	52 x 2	64 x 1	41 x 2	11 x 4
10 x 5	23 x 2	78 x 1	60 x 2	13 x 3	12 x 2	33 x 3
11 x 9	22 x 4	12 x 4	77 x 0	10 x 6	49 x 1	34 x 2
57 x 1	10 x 3	21 x 3	12 x 3	68 x 0	13 x 2	11 x 7
20 x 4	31 x 2	41 x 3	11 x 8	58 x 1	93 x 0	21 x 5

Multiplying 2-digit numbers by 1-digit numbers without regrouping

Ready to Regroup?

Sometimes you need to regroup numbers when multiplying, just as when adding.

Step 1

100	10	1
	1	
	6	4
x		3
		2

Multiply 3 x 4. Regroup 12 as two 1s and one 10. Carry the 1 to the 10s column.

Step 2

100	10	1
	1	
	6	4
x		3
1	9	2

Multiply by the 10s column (3 x 6) then add the 1 you carried over. Regroup as nine 10s and one 100 and carry the 1 to the 100s column.

Multiply. Regroup if you need to.

$$\begin{array}{r} 25 \\ \times\ 3 \end{array} \qquad \begin{array}{r} 16 \\ \times\ 4 \end{array} \qquad \begin{array}{r} 17 \\ \times\ 5 \end{array} \qquad \begin{array}{r} 43 \\ \times\ 2 \end{array} \qquad \begin{array}{r} 24 \\ \times\ 5 \end{array}$$

$$\begin{array}{r} 35 \\ \times\ 7 \end{array} \qquad \begin{array}{r} 32 \\ \times\ 4 \end{array} \qquad \begin{array}{r} 57 \\ \times\ 3 \end{array} \qquad \begin{array}{r} 17 \\ \times\ 9 \end{array} \qquad \begin{array}{r} 11 \\ \times\ 9 \end{array}$$

$$\begin{array}{r} 28 \\ \times\ 2 \end{array} \qquad \begin{array}{r} 44 \\ \times\ 3 \end{array} \qquad \begin{array}{r} 14 \\ \times\ 6 \end{array} \qquad \begin{array}{r} 81 \\ \times\ 2 \end{array} \qquad \begin{array}{r} 56 \\ \times\ 3 \end{array}$$

Painting Day

$$\overset{2}{3}4 \\ \times\ 7 \\ \overline{238}$$

Multiply. Regroup if you need to.

13 × 7	19 × 3	12 × 8	14 × 2	63 × 3
15 × 4	11 × 7	16 × 5	48 × 2	22 × 5
24 × 3	32 × 4	50 × 8	77 × 2	45 × 5
12 × 2	86 × 1	17 × 8	28 × 9	33 × 4
75 × 2	56 × 4	47 × 5	91 × 1	60 × 3

Multiplying 2-digit numbers by 1-digit numbers with and without regrouping

Daydreamer Problems

Instead of concentrating, Vince was thinking about basketball during his math test. Find Vince's mistakes and correct them.

1
2
24
x 3
62

2
19
x 3
57

32
x 3
66

2
14
x 5
72

53
x 3
179

1
45
x 2
90

21
x 6
111

3
16
x 5
85

1
38
x 2
76

62
x 5
307

1
17
x 3
41

4
36
x 4
162

3
18
x 4
72

2
27
x 2
64

40
x 5
200

1
12
x 8
86

82
x 2
164

1
46
x 3
128

7
28
x 9
182

31
x 4
124

Multiplying 2-digit numbers by 1-digit numbers with and without regrouping

Small Treats

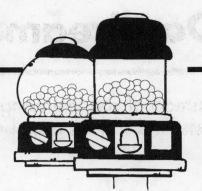

Read each problem then solve it using multiplication.
Show your work.

1. There are three gumball machines that hold 75 gumballs per machine.
   How many gumballs does it take to fill all three machines?

2. There are four mini-toy machines that hold 57 mini-toys per machine.
   How many mini-toys does it take to fill all the machines?

3. Two sour candy machines hold 98 sour candies each. How many sour
   candies does it take to fill both machines?

4. The sticker machine holds 65 stickers. It was filled four times in one week.
   How many stickers were put in the machine in that week?

5. Uh-oh! The rubber ball machine broke and all the balls spilled out!
   Three children picked up 49 balls each. How many balls did they pick
   up altogether?

6. There are five jelly bean machines that hold 86 jelly beans per machine.
   How many jelly beans does it take to fill all five machines?

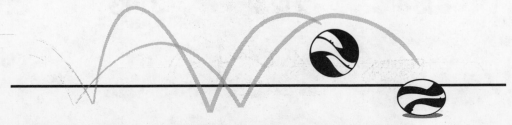

Do the Two-Step

Some division problems require more than one step.
This is called long division.

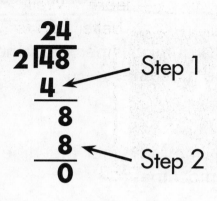

$$
\begin{array}{r}
24 \\
2\overline{)48} \\
4 \quad \leftarrow \text{Step 1}\\
\hline
8 \\
8 \quad \leftarrow \text{Step 2}\\
\hline
0
\end{array}
$$

Solve the problems using long division.

$4\overline{)88}$ $3\overline{)39}$ $3\overline{)63}$ $9\overline{)99}$ $2\overline{)64}$

$2\overline{)84}$ $5\overline{)55}$ $3\overline{)36}$ $4\overline{)84}$ $7\overline{)77}$

$1\overline{)29}$ $8\overline{)88}$ $2\overline{)28}$ $3\overline{)93}$ $2\overline{)48}$

Hop to It!

Sometimes the divisor does not go evenly into the first digit of the dividend.

```
      16
   3 )48
     -3
      18
      18
       0
```

"There's more to learn? Well, we'd better hop to it!"

Solve the problems using long division.

6)72   4)56   7)84   5)90   3)78

7)91   5)60   4)64   4)96   2)32

3)57   8)96   3)87   2)98   3)48

Remember the Remainder!

Some dividends can be split evenly by a divisor.

$5\overline{)15}$ 5 goes into **15** evenly **3** times (**5 x 3 = 15**), so $5\overline{)15}^{3}$

Some cannot.

$5\overline{)17}$ **5 x 3 = 15 < 17**

          5 x 4 = 20 > 17

When it cannot, find the closest number of times the dividend can be split by the divisor without going over the dividend and write that number in the place of the quotient.

Subtract the multiplication product from the dividend. What is left is the remainder.

$$\begin{array}{r} 3 \\ 5\overline{)17} \\ -15 \\ \hline 2 \end{array}$$

Write the answer using "r" for remainder.

$$\begin{array}{r} 3\,r\,2 \\ 5\overline{)17} \\ -15 \\ \hline 2 \end{array}$$

Solve each problem. Use multiplication to check how many times the dividend can be split by the divisor without going over the dividend.

	Multiply to check.	Write the answer.

8 ÷ 3   **3 x ___ = ___ < 8** $3\overline{)8}$

          3 x ___ = ___ > 8

11 ÷ 2   **2 x ___ = ___ < 11** $2\overline{)11}$

          2 x ___ = ___ > 11

15 ÷ 4   **4 x ___ = ___ < 15** $4\overline{)15}$

          4 x ___ = ___ > 15

Paint by Numbers

Divide. Then circle the problem with the largest remainder, mark an X on the problem with the smallest remainder, and draw a box around the problems with no remainders.

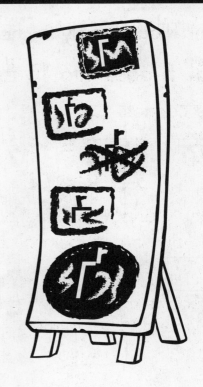

$7\overline{)29}$ $4\overline{)20}$ $5\overline{)43}$ $9\overline{)58}$ $3\overline{)23}$

$6\overline{)54}$ $7\overline{)37}$ $8\overline{)64}$ $7\overline{)62}$ $4\overline{)39}$

$8\overline{)66}$ $9\overline{)30}$ $7\overline{)42}$ $3\overline{)26}$ $6\overline{)48}$

$6\overline{)14}$ $5\overline{)24}$ $9\overline{)63}$ $86\overline{)86}$ $5\overline{)37}$

Check the Facts!

Divide. Then multiply to check your answer.

8⟌40 5	x 8 5 40	7⟌56	x 7
6⟌36	x 6	4⟌28	x 4
3⟌18	x 3	5⟌45	x 5
9⟌45	x 9	2⟌16	x 2
7⟌21	x 7	4⟌36	x 4

Checking division with multiplication

What's the Sign?

Write the missing symbol (+, −, x, ÷) to make each sentence true.

6 ⊡ 3 = 9   14 ☐ 2 = 7   9 ☐ 4 = 36

27 ☐ 9 = 3   3 ☐ 3 = 9   12 ☐ 6 = 6

4 ☐ 3 = 12   24 ☐ 4 = 6   18 ☐ 6 = 12

5 ☐ 2 = 7   13 ☐ 2 = 11   18 ☐ 4 = 22

55 ☐ 13 = 68   6 ☐ 1 = 6   72 ☐ 8 = 9

Write < or > to make each sentence true.

390 ⊡ 360   214 ☐ 204   556 ☐ 558

613 ☐ 316   481 ☐ 490   933 ☐ 929

815 ☐ 830   198 ☐ 200   343 ☐ 339

101 ☐ 110   791 ☐ 794   588 ☐ 578

A Riddle For You

Solve the problems.

247	781	197	863
+ 236	− 669	+ 149	− 256

     T   N   E   P

2795	3845	4729	6461
+ 1348	+ 1631	− 483	− 4253

     E   A   W   R

5537	4721	9529	2645
− 3319	+ 414	+ 6261	+ 218

     H   P   S   E

Match the numbers with letters above to answer the riddle.

What is black and white and read all over?

$\overline{603}$ $\overline{2218}$ $\overline{346}$ $\overline{112}$ $\overline{4143}$ $\overline{4246}$ $\overline{3268}$ $\overline{607}$ $\overline{5476}$ $\overline{5135}$ $\overline{2863}$ $\overline{2208}$

Big Numbers

Match.

3 hundreds
9 tens
3 ones

9 hundreds
3 tens
9 ones

9 hundreds
3 ones

9 hundreds
3 tens

9 hundreds
9 tens
3 ones

900 + 3

900 + 30 + 9

300 + 90 + 3

900 + 90 + 3

900 + 30

Nine hundred thirty

Nine hundred three

Nine hundred ninety-three

Nine hundred thirty-nine

Three hundred ninety-three

Rewrite the numbers in order from least to greatest.

888   887   897   891   _____ _____ _____ _____

2699   2741   2739   2693   _____ _____ _____ _____

578   575   577   557   _____ _____ _____ _____

1969   1971   1917   1996   _____ _____ _____ _____

8809   8812   8821   8800   _____ _____ _____ _____

Identifying word names for 3-digit numbers; writing 3- and 4-digit numbers in order

Number Review

Round to the nearest 100.

563 = almost _____   **1755** = almost _____   **280** = almost _____

9826 = almost _____   **8167** = almost _____   **729** = almost _____

Round to the nearest 1000.

3491 = almost _____   **1438** = almost _____   **5601** = almost _____

2982 = almost _____   **7459** = almost _____   **9199** = almost _____

Circle the odd numbers.

937	**460**	**555**	**724**	**881**	**463**
372	**111**	**296**	**693**	**449**	**112**

Write the missing symbol (+, −, x, ÷) to make each sentence true.

81 ☐ **9 = 9**   **6** ☐ **3 = 18**   **36** ☐ **9 = 4**   **49** ☐ **7 = 42**

54 ☐ **5 = 49**   **23** ☐ **8 = 31**   **45** ☐ **1 = 45**   **8** ☐ **3 = 24**

Write < or > to make each sentence true.

653 ☐ **563** $\frac{1}{3}$ ☐ $\frac{1}{2}$ **2871** ☐ **2781**   **548** ☐ **458**

$\frac{1}{2}$ ☐ $\frac{1}{4}$ **497** ☐ **498**   **1933** ☐ **1929**   **3621** ☐ **3612**

Graph It!

Show the information on each graph.

All 20 students received their final math grades. Here are the results:

5 A's

4 B's

6 C's

3 D's

2 F's

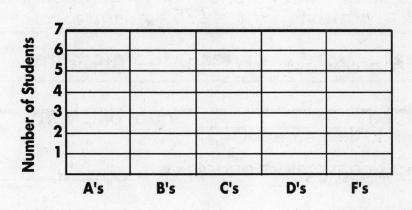

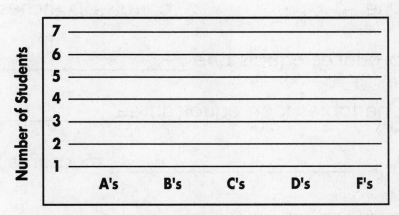

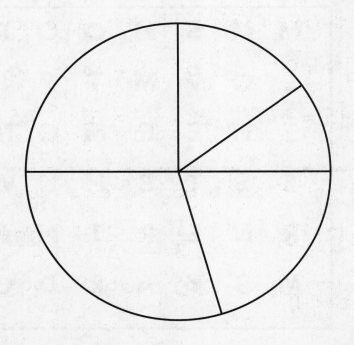

Puzzle Fun

Write a word from the box to complete each sentence. Then circle the words in the puzzle. The words can go forward, backward, or down.

feet	yard	meter	thermometer	teaspoons	pound

1. Three _____ equal one yard.

2. 100 centimeters equals one _____.

3. One _____ equals 36 inches.

4. 16 ounces equals one _____.

5. One tablespoon equals three _____.

6. A _____ measures temperature.

```
M M S N O O P S A E T
E O V M T P L K P N D
T H E R M O M E T E R
E S T B H U W P A E V
R N E R T N A T E E F
M B Y A R D O E O N S
```

Reviewing measurement units and tools

Geometry Review

Circle the correct answer.

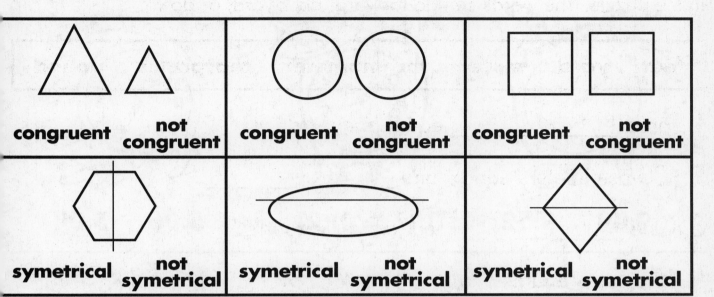

| congruent | not congruent | congruent | not congruent | congruent | not congruent |
| symetrical | not symetrical | symetrical | not symetrical | symetrical | not symetrical |

Find the area.

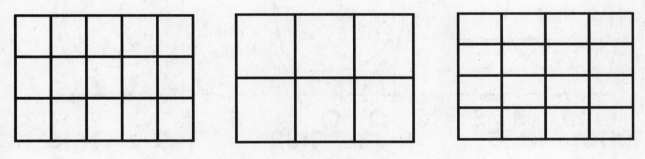

_____   _____   _____

Find the perimeter.

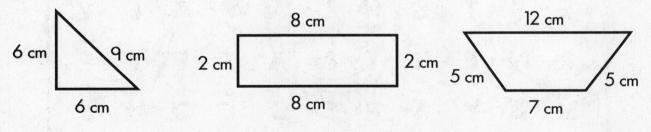

_____   _____   _____

Kitty Clocks

Circle the correct answer.

9:49   **9:52**   **11:17**   **11:21**   **5:06**   **5:04**

10:10   **10:15**   **2:32**   **1:32**   **11:21**   **11:16**

3:39   **3:29**   **7:30**   **8:30**   **4:15**   **4:11**

Telling time to the minute

Coin Riddles

Read the riddle. Circle the answers.

Josh has 24¢
in his pocket.
He has 6 coins.
What coins does
Josh have?

Kim has 30¢
in her pocket.
She has 3 coins.
What coins does
Kim have?

Matt has 16¢
in his pocket.
He has 4 coins.
What coins does
Matt have?

Jake has more than
3 nickels, but less than
2 dimes.

How much money does
Jake have?

18¢   25¢   30¢

Laura has less than
4 nickels, but more than
8 pennies.

How much money does
Laura have?

5¢   15¢   20¢

Speed Drill I

FINISH

Solve the problems as fast as you can. Time yourself or ask someone to time you.

6 × 3	9 × 2	4 × 5	8 × 9	7 × 6	5 × 5	4 × 3
8 × 3	2 × 6	5 × 9	3 × 3	9 × 7	6 × 6	5 × 2
9 × 9	7 × 8	6 × 5	8 × 6	4 × 4	8 × 8	9 × 1
2 × 5	6 × 9	4 × 6	5 × 7	4 × 8	9 × 3	2 × 2
4 × 7	9 × 4	7 × 0	8 × 1	9 × 8	6 × 7	1 × 4
7 × 8	5 × 4	7 × 2	9 × 6	2 × 3	7 × 7	9 × 5
9 × 0	6 × 4	3 × 8	2 × 4	1 × 1	7 × 3	8 × 4

Time: _____

Missed _____ out of 49

Reviewing multiplication facts

Speed Drill II

Solve the problems as fast as you can. Time yourself or ask someone to time you.

$2\overline{)12}$ $3\overline{)24}$ $4\overline{)32}$ $5\overline{)5}$ $9\overline{)81}$ $7\overline{)21}$ $5\overline{)20}$

$7\overline{)56}$ $8\overline{)48}$ $1\overline{)7}$ $9\overline{)63}$ $3\overline{)9}$ $4\overline{)24}$ $4\overline{)28}$

$5\overline{)10}$ $8\overline{)72}$ $6\overline{)24}$ $6\overline{)48}$ $8\overline{)16}$ $5\overline{)35}$ $2\overline{)8}$

$8\overline{)24}$ $3\overline{)18}$ $7\overline{)14}$ $8\overline{)56}$ $7\overline{)63}$ $3\overline{)27}$ $9\overline{)9}$

$6\overline{)42}$ $8\overline{)64}$ $5\overline{)25}$ $2\overline{)10}$ $7\overline{)49}$ $6\overline{)36}$ $7\overline{)35}$

$6\overline{)30}$ $5\overline{)40}$ $4\overline{)12}$ $9\overline{)27}$ $4\overline{)36}$ $9\overline{)72}$ $3\overline{)6}$

$6\overline{)18}$ $9\overline{)54}$ $5\overline{)15}$ $2\overline{)18}$ $9\overline{)45}$ $4\overline{)16}$ $8\overline{)32}$

Time: _____   Missed _____ out of 49

Multiply or Divide?

Read each problem. Circle M if it should be solved using multiplication or D if it should be solved using division. Then solve the problem.

Jason bought nine pizzas for his party. Each is cut into eight pieces. How many pieces are there altogether?

M D

Jason has exactly enough pizza to serve himself and each guest three pieces of pizza. Including Jason, how many people are at the party?

M D

Jason had figured that each person at the party would drink two cans of pop. How many cans of pop did Jason buy?

M D

Jason bought three ice cream cakes. How many pieces must he cut from each cake for everyone to have a piece?

M D

One of the cakes was made with vanilla ice cream. The other two are chocolate. How many pieces of chocolate ice cream cake did Jason serve?

M D

Jason received one gift from each of his friends at the party. How many gifts did Jason get?

M D

Answer Key

Please take time to review the work your child has completed and remember to praise both success and effort. If your child makes a mistake, let him or her know that mistakes are a part of learning. Then explain the correct answer and how to find it. Taking the time to help your child and an active interest in his or her progress shows that you feel learning is important.

page 1

Math Splash

Help the frog get to the pond by solving the problem on each rock.

38 + 15 = **53**	47 − 18 = **29**	19 + 34 = **53**
90 − 51 = **39**	58 − 42 = **16**	44 + 26 = **70**
24 + 55 = **79**	23 − 17 = **6**	41 − 21 = **20**
	63 + 37 = **100**	

Adding and subtracting 2-digit numbers   1

page 2

Four at a Time

Add.

When adding more than two numbers, look for easy combinations first.

7 + 2 + 3 + 4 = **16**

6 8 2 +4 = **20**	3 3 8 +7 = **16**	5 5 3 +3 = **15**	1 6 9 +5 = **21**	2 9 4 +8 = **23**
4 7 6 +0 = **18**	7 3 5 +1 = **22**	3 9 1 +0 = **14**	3 6 7 +2 = **17**	9 8 7 +3 = **26**
5 5 5 +5 = **20**	6 4 4 +5 = **19**	3 7 8 +5 = **23**	7 7 7 +7 = **28**	7 7 7 +4 = **24**

Adding four 1-digit numbers   2

page 3

Number Sleuth

Solve the riddles.

I have 4 tens, 7 hundreds, and 6 ones. What number am I? **746** A	I have 3 ones, 9 hundreds, and 2 tens. What number am I? **923**
I have the same number of hundreds, tens, and ones. I have 4 tens. What number am I? **444**	I have the same number of hundreds, tens, and ones. I have 1 one. What number am I? **111** H
I have 4 ones and 1 ten. I am between 610 and 620. What number am I? **614**	I have 3 tens and 9 ones. I am between 500 and 600. What number am I? **539**
I have 8 ones and 2 hundreds. I am between 270 and 280. What number am I? **278**	I have 5 hundreds and 3 ones. I am more than 590. What number am I? **593**

Match the numbers with letters above to answer the riddle.

What goes through a door, but never goes in or out?

A K E Y H O L E
746 614 923 593 111 278 444

Solving riddles with 3-digit numbers   3

page 4
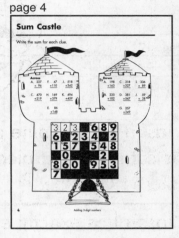

Sum Castle

Write the sum for each clue.

Across / Down crossnumber puzzle

Adding 3-digit numbers   4

page 5

Token Trade In

Read each problem. Write a number sentence and solve.

1. Manuel bought a truck and markers. How many tokens did he spend?
409 + 129 = 538

2. Hunter has 390 tokens. He bought a coloring book. How many tokens does he have left?
390 − 197 = 193

3. Kameisha bought a doll and stickers. How many tokens did she spend?
249 + 106 = 355

4. Nick bought stickers and a sticker book. How many tokens did he spend?
106 + 225 = 331

5. Liza has 540 tokens. She bought a sticker book. How many tokens does she have left?
540 − 225 = 315

6. Mai bought a stuffed bear and a coloring book. How many tokens did she spend?
470 + 197 = 667

7. Seth has 425 tokens. He bought a coloring book. How many tokens does he have left?
425 − 409 = 16

8. Jenna has 350 tokens. She bought a doll. How many tokens does she have left?
350 − 249 = 101

9. Suzy bought a coloring book and a doll. How many tokens did she spend?
225 + 249 = 474

10. Tucker has 639 tokens. He bought a stuffed bear. How many tokens does he have left?
639 − 470 = 169

Solving addition and subtraction word problems involving 3-digit numbers   5

page 6
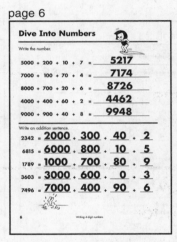

Dive Into Numbers

Write the number.

5000 + 200 + 10 + 7 = **5217**
7000 + 100 + 70 + 4 = **7174**
8000 + 700 + 20 + 6 = **8726**
4000 + 400 + 60 + 2 = **4462**
9000 + 900 + 40 + 8 = **9948**

Write an addition sentence.

2342 = **2000** + **300** + **40** + **2**
6815 = **6000** + **800** + **10** + **5**
1789 = **1000** + **700** + **80** + **9**
3603 = **3000** + **600** + **0** + **3**
7496 = **7000** + **400** + **90** + **6**

Writing 4-digit numbers   6

page 7

Name Game

Write the number.

One thousand, two hundred eleven = **1,211**
Eight thousand, thirty-five = **8,035**
Seven thousand, one hundred = **7,100**
Five thousand, four hundred twenty-three = **5,423**
Nine thousand, five hundred seventeen = **9,517**
Two thousand, seven hundred thirty-four = **2,734**
Two thousand, eight hundred nine = **2,809**
Five thousand, three hundred forty-two = **5,342**
Six thousand, nine hundred sixty-one = **6,961**
Four thousand, two hundred ninety = **4,290**
Three thousand, one hundred seventy-five = **3,175**
Four thousand, six hundred fifty-seven = **4,657**
Nine thousand = **9,000**
Three thousand, four hundred thirty-two = **3,432**
Four thousand, two hundred nine = **4,209**

Identifying word names for 4-digit numbers   7

page 8

Adding Thousands

Add. Circle the sums that are greater than 6000. What pattern do you see?

2346 + 3754 = (6100)	2935 + 1263 = 4198	3024 + 3126 = (6150)	4147 + 2053 = (6200)
3152 + 1756 = 4908	3125 + 3125 = (6250)	1246 + 1725 = 2971	1168 + 5132 = (6300)
2132 + 4218 = (6350)	3049 + 2743 = 5792	5143 + 1257 = (6400)	2914 + 2279 = 5193
4373 + 1612 = 5985	1221 + 5229 = (6450)	2936 + 3564 = (6500)	4680 + 1299 = 5979
3035 + 3515 = (6550)	1794 + 1179 = 2973	2605 + 2236 = 4841	4237 + 2363 = (6600)

sums increase by 50   8

page 9

Subtracting Thousands

Find the difference.

4321 − 1218 = 3103	5619 − 2804 = 2815	9846 − 4373 = 5473	6527 − 2213 = 4314
7049 − 3528 = 3521	3267 − 1742 = 1525	8473 − 2439 = 6034	5742 − 1812 = 3930
6836 − 2724 = 4112	2799 − 1982 = 817	4954 − 1426 = 3528	7821 − 2816 = 5005
5431 − 2161 = 3270	8862 − 1215 = 7647	3961 − 2820 = 1141	9789 − 3299 = 6490
3776 − 1349 = 2427	7449 − 2623 = 4826	6675 − 2231 = 4444	5859 − 4182 = 1677

Subtracting 4-digit numbers   9

page 10

Odds and Evens

Color the **odd** numbered balls blue.
Color the **even** numbered balls yellow.

377 864
552 483 729 606
435 207 538 780
198 236 367 811
412 555 992 803

Identifying odd and even numbers   10

page 11
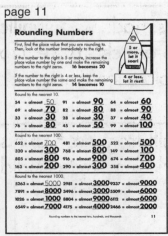

Rounding Numbers

First, find the place value that you are rounding to. Then, look at the number immediately to the right.

If the number to the right is 5 or more, increase the place value number by one and make the remaining numbers to the right zeros. 16 becomes 20

If the number to the right is 4 or less, keep the place value number the same and make the remaining numbers to the right zeros. 14 becomes 10

Round to the nearest 10.
54 = almost **50**   91 = almost **90**   64 = almost **60**
69 = almost **70**   82 = almost **80**   88 = almost **90**
33 = almost **30**   37 = almost **40**
76 = almost **80**   45 = almost **50**   99 = almost **100**

Round to the nearest 100.
652 = almost **700**   481 = almost **500**   522 = almost **500**
320 = almost **300**   768 = almost **800**   149 = almost **100**
805 = almost **800**   904 = almost **900**   705 = almost **700**
163 = almost **200**   290 = almost **300**   358 = almost **400**

Round to the nearest 1000.
5263 = almost **5000**   2981 = almost **3000**   9237 = almost **9000**
7891 = almost **8000**   3496 = almost **3000**   5509 = almost **6000**
1026 = almost **1000**   8804 = almost **9000**   6112 = almost **6000**
6549 = almost **7000**   4175 = almost **4000**   2466 = almost **2000**

Rounding numbers to the nearest tens, hundreds, and thousands   11

page 12
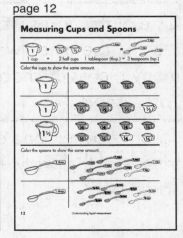

Measuring Cups and Spoons

1 cup = 2 half cups   1 tablespoon (tbsp.) = 3 teaspoons (tsp.)

Color the cups to show the same amount.

Color the spoons to show the same amount.

Understanding liquid measurement   12

Answers

61

Pounds and Ounces

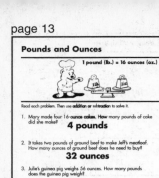

1 pound (lb.) = 16 ounces (oz.)

Read each problem. Then use **addition** or **subtraction** to solve it.

1. Mary made four 16-ounce cakes. How many pounds of cake did she make?
4 pounds

2. It takes two pounds of ground beef to make Jeff's meatloaf. How many ounces of ground beef does he need to buy?
32 ounces

3. Julie's guinea pig weighs 56 ounces. How many pounds does the guinea pig weigh?
3 ½ pounds

4. Zack's backpack weighs 48 ounces. He removed his math book, which weighs one pound. How much does his backpack weigh now?
2 pounds or 32 ounces

Understanding pounds and ounces; solving word problems   13

Feet, Yards, and Meters

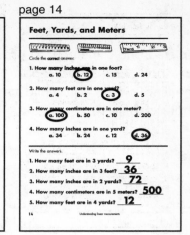

Circle the correct answer.
1. How many inches are in one foot?
a. 10   **b. 12**   c. 15   d. 24

2. How many feet are in one yard?
a. 4   b. 2   **c. 3**   d. 5

3. How many centimeters are in one meter?
a. 100   b. 50   c. 10   d. 200

4. How many inches are in one yard?
a. 34   b. 24   c. 12   **d. 36**

Write the answers.
1. How many feet are in 3 yards? **9**
2. How many inches are in 3 feet? **36**
3. How many inches are in 2 yards? **72**
4. How many centimeters are in 5 meters? **500**
5. How many feet are in 4 yards? **12**

14   Understanding linear measurements

Same Size

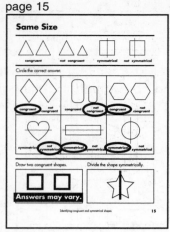

congruent   not congruent   symmetrical   not symmetrical

Circle the correct answer.

congruent / not congruent

symmetrical / not symmetrical

Draw two congruent shapes.   Divide the shape symmetrically.

Answers may vary.

Identifying congruent and symmetrical shapes   15

Area and Perimeter

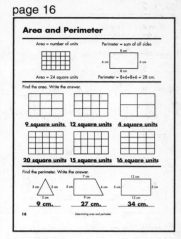

Area = number of units   Perimeter = sum of all sides

Area = 24 square units   Perimeter = 8+6+8+6 = 28 cm.

Find the area. Write the answer.

9 square units   **12 square units**   **4 square units**

20 square units   **15 square units**   **16 square units**

Find the perimeter. Write the answer.

9 cm.   **27 cm.**   **34 cm.**

16   Determining area and perimeter

Comparing Fractions

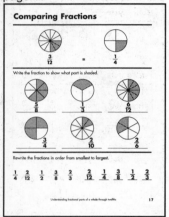

$\frac{3}{12}$ = $\frac{1}{4}$

Write the fraction to show what part is shaded.

$\frac{5}{8}$ $\frac{1}{3}$ $\frac{6}{12}$

$\frac{3}{4}$ $\frac{2}{10}$ $\frac{2}{6}$

Rewrite the fractions in order from smallest to largest.

$\frac{1}{4}$ $\frac{2}{12}$ $\frac{1}{2}$ $\frac{3}{8}$ $\frac{2}{3}$ $\frac{2}{12}$ $\frac{1}{4}$ $\frac{3}{8}$ $\frac{1}{2}$ $\frac{2}{3}$

Understanding fractional parts of a whole through twelfths   17

How's the Weather?

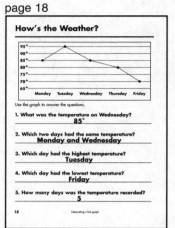

Use the graph to answer the questions.

1. What was the temperature on Wednesday?
85°

2. Which two days had the same temperature?
Monday and Wednesday

3. Which day had the highest temperature?
Tuesday

4. Which day had the lowest temperature?
Friday

5. How many days was the temperature recorded?
5

18   Interpreting a line graph

Favorite Subject

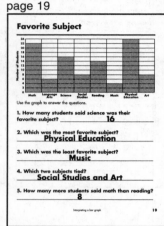

Use the graph to answer the questions.

1. How many students said science was their favorite subject? **16**

2. Which was the most favorite subject?
Physical Education

3. Which was the least favorite subject?
Music

4. Which two subjects tied?
Social Studies and Art

5. How many more students said math than reading?
8

Interpreting a bar graph   19

Favorite Sport

14 football   9 basketball   7 track   12 soccer   10 baseball   8 volleyball

Each student named one sport. Use the graph to answer the questions.

1. Which was the most favorite sport? **football**

2. Which was the least favorite sport? **track**

3. How many students named a favorite sport? **60**

4. How many students said volleyball? **8**

5. How many more students said soccer than basketball? **2**

6. What fraction of students said football? **$\frac{1}{4}$**

20   Interpreting a circle graph

Temperature

Use the thermometer to answer the questions.

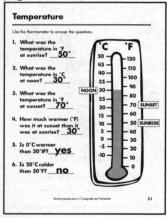

1. What was the temperature in °F at sunrise? **50°**

2. What was the temperature in °C at noon? **30°**

3. What was the temperature in °F at sunset? **70°**

4. How much warmer (°F) was it at sunset than it was at sunrise? **30°**

5. Is 0°C warmer than 20°F? **yes**

6. Is 20°C colder than 50°F? **no**

Reading temperature in Centigrade and Fahrenheit   21

Robot Time

Write the time.

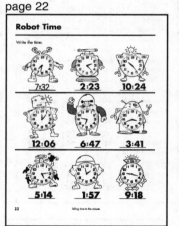

7:32   **2:23**   **10:24**

12:06   **6:47**   **3:41**

5:14   **1:57**   **9:18**

22   Telling time to the minute

Summer Time Fun

Read each problem. Write the answer.

Eric left home at 11 o'clock. It took 1½ hours to get to the beach. What time did Eric get to the beach?
12:30

Kate goes to camp at 11 a.m. Pat goes to camp at 1 p.m. Who goes to camp first?
Kate

Samir got to the park at 2:45 p.m. He went home at 5 p.m. How long was Samir at the park?
2 hrs. 15 min.

The soccer game starts at 6 o'clock. It ends one and a quarter hours later. What time does the soccer game end?
7:15

Meg left home at 9 o'clock. It took her 2½ hours to get to Aunt Lynn's. What time did Meg get to Aunt Lynn's?
11:30

Ben went to the pool at 2:00. He stayed for 3 hours and 35 minutes. What time did Ben get home?
5:35

Solving word problems that involve time   23

In the Bank

Count the money. Write the amount.

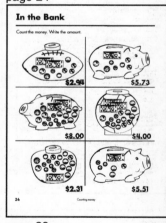

$2.94   **$5.73**

$8.00   **$4.00**

$2.31   **$5.51**

24   Counting money

How Much Money?

Solve the problems.

Rosa has $10.00. She bought a dress for $8.64. How much money does she have left?
$10.00 − 8.64   **$1.36**

Howard has $7.50. He wants to buy a video that costs $9.00. How much money does he need to save?
$9.00 − 7.50   **$1.50**

Todd has $8.78. He bought a football for $7.97. How much money does he have left?
$8.78 − 7.97   **81¢**

Jill has $6.85. She wants to buy a purse that costs $10.00. How much money does she need to save?
$10.00 − 6.85   **$3.15**

Paul has $9.20. He bought a hat for $5.91. How much money does he have left?
$9.20 − 5.91   **$3.29**

Solving word problems that involve money   25

Put a Name to the Number

Factors are the numbers you use to multiply. A **product** is the answer you get when you multiply factors together.

Factor   Factor   Product
2   x   3   =   6

Whenever you multiply a factor by the number 1, the product is equal to that factor.

Factor   Factor   Product
3   x   1   =   3

Multiply to find the product.
1x9 = **9**   2x1 = **2**   1x5 = **5**   7x1 = **7**
3x1 = **3**   1x1 = **1**   4x2 = **8**   9x1 = **9**
8x1 = **8**   2x2 = **4**   1x4 = **4**   2x6 = **12**
1x2 = **2**   5x2 = **10**   6x1 = **6**   7x2 = **14**
2x8 = **16**   1x8 = **8**   1x3 = **3**   1x6 = **6**
3x2 = **6**   9x2 = **18**   5x1 = **5**   2x7 = **14**

26   Understanding multiplication; practicing multiplication facts

Find the Perfect Fit

Write the missing factors.

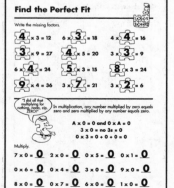

4 x 3 = 12   6 x **3** = 18   4 x **4** = 16
3 x 9 = 27   **4** x 5 = 20   4 x **3** = 12
6 x **4** = 24   **5** x 3 = 15   **8** x 3 = 24
9 x 4 = 36   **7** x 3 = 21   3 x **2** = 6

"I did all that multiplying for nothing, nada, zip, ZERO!"

In multiplication, any number multiplied by zero equals zero and zero multiplied by any number equals zero.

A x 0 = 0 and 0 x A = 0
3 x 0 = 0 no 3s = 0
0 x 3 = 0 + 0 + 0 = 0

Multiply.
7x0 = **0**   2x0 = **0**   0x5 = **0**   0x1 = **0**
0x6 = **0**   0x4 = **0**   3x0 = **0**   9x0 = **0**
8x0 = **0**   0x7 = **0**   4x0 = **0**   1x0 = **0**

Practicing multiplication facts   27

Two of a Kind

In multiplication, A x B is equal to B x A.

A x B = B x A
3 x 5 = 5 x 3   3 x 5 = 15
5 x 3 = 15

Rewrite the factors to show that A x B equals B x A. Then solve the problems.

5 x 6 = **6** x **5** = 30   6 x 3 = **3** x **6** = 18
4 x 5 = **5** x **4** = 20   2 x 6 = **6** x **2** = 12
6 x 4 = **4** x **6** = 24   6 x 7 = **7** x **6** = 42
5 x 2 = **2** x **5** = 10   7 x 5 = **5** x **7** = 35
8 x 6 = **6** x **8** = 48   9 x 5 = **5** x **9** = 45
5 x 8 = **8** x **5** = 40   6 x 9 = **9** x **6** = 54

28   Practicing multiplication facts

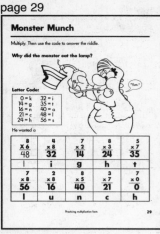

Monster Munch

Multiply. Then use the code to answer the riddle.

Why did the monster eat the lamp?

Letter Code:
0 = k, 32 = i, 14 = m, 36 = a, 16 = n, 40 = o, 21 = c, 48 = l, 24 = h, 56 = s

He wanted a

| 8 ×6 = 48 | 4 ×8 = 32 | 7 ×2 = 14 | 8 ×3 = 24 | 5 ×7 = 35 |
| i | g | h | t | |

| 7 ×8 = 56 | 2 ×8 = 16 | 8 ×5 = 40 | 3 ×7 = 21 | 7 ×0 = 0 |
| l | u | n | c | h |

Practicing multiplication facts   29

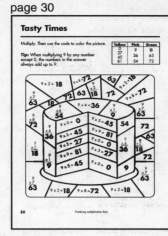

Tasty Times

Multiply. Then use the code to color the picture.

Tip: When multiplying 9 by any number except 0, the numbers in the answer always add up to 9.

	Yellow	Pink	Green
0	9	18
27	36	63
45	54	72
81		

Practicing multiplication facts   30

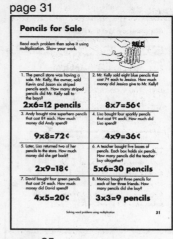

Pencils for Sale

Read each problem then solve it using multiplication. Show your work.

1. The pencil store was having a sale. Mr. Kelly, the owner, sold Kevin and Jason six each. How many striped pencils did Mr. Kelly sell to the boys?
2×6=12 pencils

2. Mr. Kelly sold eight blue pencils that cost 7¢ each to Jessica. How much money did Jessica give to Mr. Kelly?
8×7=56¢

3. Andy bought nine superhero pencils that cost 8¢ each. How much money did Andy spend?
9×8=72¢

4. Lisa bought four sparkly pencils that cost 9¢ each. How much did Lisa spend?
4×9=36¢

5. Later, Lisa returned two of her pencils to the store. How much money did she get back?
2×9=18¢

6. A teacher bought five boxes of pencils. Each box holds six pencils. How many pencils did the teacher buy altogether?
5×6=30 pencils

7. David bought four green pencils that cost 5¢ each. How much money did David spend?
4×5=20¢

8. Monica bought three pencils for each of her three friends. How many pencils did she buy?
3×3=9 pencils

Solving word problems using multiplication   31

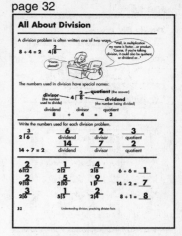

All About Division

A division problem is often written one of two ways.
$8 ÷ 4 = 2$ $4\overline{)8}$

The numbers used in division have special names.

divisor (the number used to divide)   quotient (the answer) $4\overline{)8}$ dividend (the number being divided)

dividend ÷ divisor = quotient
8 ÷ 4 = 2

Write the numbers used for each division problem.

| $2\overline{)6}$ | $6\overline{)14}$ | $2\overline{)4}$ |
| dividend 6 | divisor 14 | quotient 2 |

14 ÷ 7 = 2
| dividend 14 | divisor 7 | quotient 2 |

$6\overline{)12}$	$2\overline{)2}$	$2\overline{)8}$	6 ÷ 6 = 1
$9\overline{)18}$	$2\overline{)10}$	$1\overline{)9}$	14 ÷ 2 = 7
$2\overline{)6}$	$5\overline{)15}$	$2\overline{)4}$	8 ÷ 1 = 8

Understanding division; practicing division facts   32

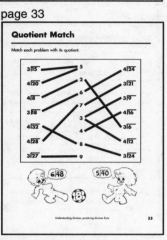

Quotient Match

Match each problem with its quotient.

$3\overline{)15}$ 5
$4\overline{)20}$ 2
$4\overline{)8}$
$3\overline{)18}$
$4\overline{)32}$ 4
$4\overline{)28}$
$3\overline{)27}$ 9

$4\overline{)24}$
$3\overline{)21}$
$3\overline{)9}$
$4\overline{)16}$
$3\overline{)6}$
$4\overline{)12}$
$3\overline{)24}$

$6\overline{)48}$ $5\overline{)40}$

Understanding division; practicing division facts   33

Division is Tee-rrific!

Divide. Then use the code to answer the riddle.

Letter Code:
1 = i, 4 = h, 7 = s
2 = d, 5 = l, 8 = t
3 = o, 6 = n, 9 = u

Why did the golfer change her socks?

| S | h | e | | h | a | d |
| 8 ×6=48 | 5 ×20 | 5 ×35 | | 4 ×24 | 4 ×92 | 6 ×12 |

| a | | h | o | l | e |
| 9 ×27 | | 4 ×35 | 3 ×18 | 5 ×25 | 2 ×14 |

| i | n | | o | n | e |
| 3 ×3 | 1 ×6 | | 3 ×3 | 4 ×24 | 4 ×28 |

Understanding division; practicing division facts   34

Divissssssssion!

Divide.

$7\overline{)8}$	$8\overline{)1}$	$7\overline{)2}$	
$7\overline{)21}$	$8\overline{)12}$	$7\overline{)14}$	$8\overline{)64}$	$7\overline{)14}$
$8\overline{)24}$	$7\overline{)7}$	$8\overline{)40}$	$7\overline{)63}$	$8\overline{)48}$
$7\overline{)35}$	$8\overline{)72}$	$7\overline{)42}$	$8\overline{)56}$	$7\overline{)42}$

Match each multiplication fact with the correct division fact.

8 × 4 $7\overline{)49}$
7 × 7 $8\overline{)32}$
7 × 9 $8\overline{)48}$
8 × 6 $7\overline{)63}$
7 × 5 $5\overline{)35}$

Practicing division and multiplication facts   35

Math Mysteries

Find the quotient.

$6\overline{)54}$	$7\overline{)63}$	$9\overline{)45}$	
$9\overline{)81}$	$3\overline{)27}$	$9\overline{)9}$	$2\overline{)18}$	$9\overline{)72}$
$9\overline{)45}$	$9\overline{)54}$	$4\overline{)36}$	$9\overline{)63}$	$9\overline{)27}$

Find the dividend.

| $9\overline{)27}$ | $6\overline{)54}$ | $2\overline{)18}$ | $9\overline{)72}$ | $4\overline{)36}$ |
| $9\overline{)81}$ | $9\overline{)45}$ | $7\overline{)63}$ | $6\overline{)54}$ | $9\overline{)9}$ |

Find the divisor.

| $9\overline{)81}$ | $9\overline{)54}$ | $3\overline{)27}$ | $9\overline{)72}$ | $5\overline{)45}$ |
| $4\overline{)36}$ | $9\overline{)18}$ | $1\overline{)9}$ | $9\overline{)63}$ | $6\overline{)54}$ |

Practicing division facts   36

Fun at School

Read each problem then solve it using division. Show your work.

1. Sarah jump roped for 21 hours in seven days. If she jumped the same amount of time every day, how many hours of jump roping did she do each day?
42÷6=7 races

2. At the school fair, 42 children want to run in the egg and spoon race. Only six children can race at a time. How many races will it take for everyone to have a turn?
21÷7=3 races

3. The school has 54 children who want to play stickball. If there can only be nine players on each team, how many teams must be formed?
54÷9=6 teams

4. Mrs. Williams has made 40 candy apples to sell. If she sells eight every hour, how many hours will it take for her to sell them all?
40÷8=5 hours

5. There are 36 children who want their faces painted at the fair. Mrs. Adams, the face painter, can paint nine faces in one hour. How many hours will it take for her to paint all 36 children?
36÷9=4 hours

6. The children in Mr. Grandy's class love sweets. The class ate 24 sticks of cotton candy. Since they ate four sticks every hour, how many hours did it take to eat all 24?
24÷4=6 hours

7. Mrs. Winkle gave out 49 stickers to seven students. If every student was given the same number of stickers, how many did each student receive?
49÷7=7 stickers

8. There are 18 students in the school orchestra. If every two students share one music stand, how many music stands are there altogether?
18÷2=9 music stands

Solving word problems using division   37

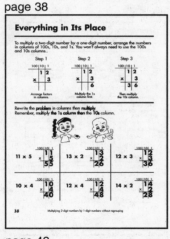

Everything in Its Place

To multiply a two-digit number by a one-digit number, arrange the numbers in columns of 100s, 10s, and 1s. You won't always need to use the 100s and 10s columns.

Step 1 — Arrange factors in columns.
Step 2 — Multiply the 1s column first.
Step 3 — Then multiply the 10s column.

Rewrite the problem in columns then multiply. Remember, multiply the 1s column then the 10s column.

| 11 × 5 = 55 | 13 × 2 = 26 | 12 × 3 = 36 |
| 10 × 4 = 40 | 12 × 4 = 48 | 14 × 2 = 28 |

Multiplying 2-digit numbers by 1-digit numbers without regrouping   38

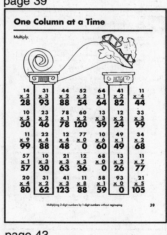

One Column at a Time

Multiply.

14 ×2 = 28	31 ×3 = 93	44 ×2 = 88	52 ×1 = 52	64 ×1 = 64	41 ×2 = 82	11 ×4 = 44
10 ×5 = 50	23 ×2 = 46	13 ×6 = 78	20 ×6 = 120	13 ×1 = 13	12 ×2 = 24	33 ×3 = 99
11 ×9 = 99	22 ×4 = 88	12 ×4 = 48	77 ×0 = 0	10 ×6 = 60	49 ×1 = 49	34 ×2 = 68
57 ×1 = 57	10 ×3 = 30	21 ×3 = 63	12 ×3 = 36	68 ×0 = 0	13 ×2 = 26	11 ×7 = 77
20 ×4 = 80	31 ×2 = 62	41 ×3 = 123	11 ×8 = 88	58 ×1 = 58	93 ×0 = 0	21 ×5 = 105

Multiplying 2-digit numbers by 1-digit numbers without regrouping   39

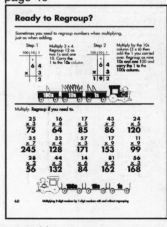

Ready to Regroup?

Sometimes you need to regroup numbers when multiplying, just as when adding.

Step 1 — Multiply 3 × 4. Regroup 12 as two 1s and one 10. Carry the 1 to the 10s column.
Step 2 — Multiply by the 10s column (3 × 6) then add the 1 you carried. Regroup as nine 10s and one 100 and carry the 1 to the 100s column.

Multiply. Regroup if you need to.

25 ×3 = 75	16 ×4 = 64	17 ×5 = 85	43 ×2 = 86	24 ×5 = 120
35 ×7 = 245	32 ×4 = 128	57 ×3 = 171	51 ×3 = 153	11 ×9 = 99
28 ×2 = 56	44 ×3 = 132	21 ×4 = 84	81 ×2 = 162	56 ×3 = 168

Multiplying 2-digit numbers by 1-digit numbers with and without regrouping   40

Painting Day

$\begin{array}{r}34 \\ ×7 \\ \hline 238\end{array}$

Multiply. Regroup if you need to.

13 ×7 = 91	19 ×3 = 57	16 ×6 = 96	14 ×2 = 28	63 ×3 = 189
15 ×4 = 60	11 ×7 = 77	16 ×5 = 80	48 ×2 = 96	22 ×5 = 110
24 ×3 = 72	32 ×4 = 128	50 ×8 = 400	77 ×2 = 154	45 ×5 = 225
12 ×2 = 24	86 ×1 = 86	17 ×8 = 136	28 ×9 = 252	33 ×4 = 132
75 ×2 = 150	56 ×4 = 224	47 ×1 = 47	91 ×1 = 91	60 ×3 = 180

Multiplying 2-digit numbers by 1-digit numbers with and without regrouping   41

Daydreamer Problems

Instead of concentrating, Vince was thinking about basketball during his math test. Find Vince's mistakes and correct them.

Multiplying 2-digit numbers by 1-digit numbers with and without regrouping   42

Small Treats

Read each problem then solve it using multiplication. Show your work.

1. There are three gumball machines that hold 75 gumballs per machine. How many gumballs does it take to fill all three machines?
75×3=225 gumballs

2. There are four mini-toy machines that hold 57 mini-toys per machine. How many mini-toys does it take to fill all four machines?
57×4=228 mini-toys

3. Two sour candy machines hold 98 sour candies each. How many sour candies does it take to fill both machines?
98×2=196 candies

4. The sticker machine holds 65 stickers. It was filled four times in one week. How many stickers were put in the machine in that week?
65×4=260 stickers

5. Uh-oh! The rubber ball machine broke and all the balls spilled out! Three children picked up 49 balls each. How many balls did they pick up altogether?
49×3=147 balls

6. There are five jelly bean machines that hold 86 jelly beans per machine. How many jelly beans does it take to fill all five machines?
86×5=430 jelly beans

Solving word problems using multiplication   43

Do the Two-Step

Some division problems require more than one step. This is called long division.

$\begin{array}{r}24 \\ 2\overline{)48} \\ -4 \\ \hline 8 \\ -8 \\ \hline 0\end{array}$
Step 1 / Step 2

Solve the problems using long division.

22 $4\overline{)88}$	13 $3\overline{)39}$	21 $3\overline{)63}$	11 $9\overline{)99}$	32 $2\overline{)64}$
42 $2\overline{)84}$	11 $4\overline{)44}$	12 $3\overline{)36}$	21 $4\overline{)84}$	11 $7\overline{)77}$
29 $1\overline{)29}$	11 $8\overline{)88}$	14 $4\overline{)56}$	31 $3\overline{)93}$	24 $2\overline{)48}$

Solving problems using long division   44

Answers

63

Hop to It!

Remember the Remainder!
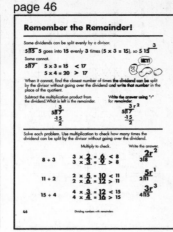

Paint by Numbers

Check the Facts!

What's the Sign?

A Riddle For You

Big Numbers

Number Review
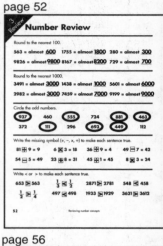

Graph It!
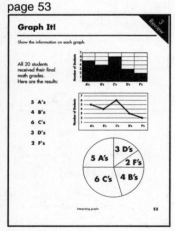

Puzzle Fun

Geometry Review
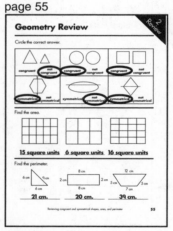

Kitty Clocks
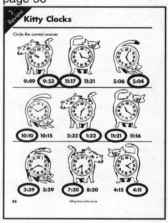

Coin Riddles
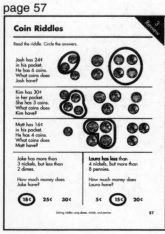

Speed Drill I

Speed Drill II

Multiply or Divide?